MIDDLE EASTERN COOKING

Beryl Frank

Thanks to all who tasted and tried the new flavors of Middle Eastern cooking from yoghurt bread to lemon-flavored chicken wings—and especially to Lou.

contents

introduction

The Middle East, as used in this book, is not a specific geographical delineation. Borders of individual countries do not change food styles. There is a similarity of dishes from Iran to Israel, from Egypt to Turkey. For this reason, pita bread is found all over the area known as the Middle East. Rice is a staple and you're sure to find pine nuts and almonds as well as all forms of the plentiful lamb and mutton.

In this collection, you are sure to find some new taste delights and unusual combinations. Don't be afraid to try them. All of the ingredients included here may be found at any store which specializes in foods of the Middle East.

Explore a store that specializes in Middle Eastern foods. You will discover exotic names like tahini, filo, dolmas, pignolia, and many other ingredients for cooking used in another part of the world. You can add to your own international cuisine by exploring the taste delights of that part of the world and including some of them on your own menus.

A word about oils. Olive oil is plentiful in the Middle East and used for most things. If you prefer, you can substitute your favorite cooking oil and it will not appreciably change the flavor of the foods. The same thing is true where butter is included in a recipe. For the most part, margarine may be substituted safely wherever butter is called for.

Spelling has been another problem. For instance, filo is frequently spelled as *phyllo*. Either is correct. Tahina has been seen spelled *tachina*. Either way, it is still sesame-seed paste. Where possible, the English words for the ingredients have been used and the spelling chosen is that which is most often found.

If this is your first venture into ethnic cooking, you may need to shop around for some ingredients. Most recipes used in this book call for ingredients available in any food store. A few, however, may take you to that special Middle Eastern store. Go, like Columbus, and explore a new world.

appetizers

fried cauliflower

**1 medium cauliflower,
  separated into florets
1 well-beaten egg seasoned with
  a pinch of salt
Oil for deep frying**

Precook the cauliflower in ½ cup boiling water until almost tender, no more than 10 minutes. Drain and pat dry with towels.

Heat cooking oil in skillet. Dip florets in the beaten egg mixture, a few at a time, and fry in the hot oil until golden on all sides. Drain on paper towels. When all are cooked, serve with garlic yoghurt sauce. Makes 4 to 8 servings.

garlic-yoghurt sauce

**1 cup unflavored yoghurt
1 medium garlic clove, crushed
¼ teaspoon salt**

Mix these ingredients together until well-blended. Taste to adjust seasonings if needed. Chill until ready to serve.

fried cauliflower

chopped liver pâté

stuffed clams

turkish meatballs

6

chopped liver pâté

¼ pound butter or chicken fat
1 large onion, finely-chopped
1 pound chicken livers

1 tablespoon Worcestershire
    sauce
Salt and pepper to taste

Melt butter or chicken fat in medium skillet; lightly tan chopped onion. Add chicken livers; cook until they are slightly pink at the center, about 5 minutes. Remove from heat.

Put entire mixture through a food mill so it is ground very smooth. If you use a colander instead of a food mill, you may want to put the liver mixture through twice to ensure a smooth texture. Last, add Worcestershire sauce and salt and pepper. Mix together well with a spoon.

Shape into a greased mold for a party. Turn out on a serving plate and surround with party crackers so that guests may help themselves. Makes 10 to 16 servings.

stuffed clams

2 dozen clams (little-neck or
    rock)
¾ cup dry white wine
¼ cup water
½ teaspoon salt
3 tablespoons olive oil
½ cup chopped onion

½ cup raw long-grain rice
¼ teaspoon pepper
½ teaspoon allspice
¼ teaspoon cinnamon
3 tablespoons currants
3 tablespoons pine nuts
2 tablespoons chopped parsley

Scrub the clams and soak them in several changes of cold water to remove the sand. Place in a skillet with the wine, water, and salt. Cover and steam for 10 minutes, until the shells open. Discard any clams that do not open. Cool and then remove the clams from the shells. Save the shells and strain the pan juices.

In a medium saucepan heat the oil and sauté the onion until golden. Add the rice and 1 cup of the pan juices. Bring to a boil. Cover and reduce the heat to low. Cook for 15 minutes. Add the pepper, spices, currants, pine nuts, and parsley. Cook for 5 minutes. Cool.

Dice the clams and add to the pilaf.

Stuff shells with the rice mixture and chill. Serve as an appetizer. Makes 24 appetizers.

turkish meatballs

1 pound lean ground lamb or
    beef
1 medium onion,
    finely-chopped
¼ cup uncooked rice
1 tablespoon salt

½ teaspoon freshly-ground
    black pepper
2 cups water
1 cup olive oil or vegetable oil
2 lightly-beaten eggs

Blend meat, onions, rice, salt, and pepper. When thoroughly mixed, form balls about 1 inch in diameter.

In a heavy skillet bring 2 cups of water to a boil. Add meatballs and return to boiling. Then simmer, uncovered, for 30 minutes, adding boiling water if needed. Remove meatballs to a plate.

Drain water from skillet and heat oil. Dip the waiting meatballs into the beaten egg and deep-fry for 5 minutes or until brown on all sides. Drain on paper towels and keep warm until ready to serve. These may be served on wooden skewers. Makes about 16 meatballs.

manna cheese

1 cup cream cheese
½ cup cream
½ teaspoon coriander seed
Honey to taste

Soften the cream cheese and blend in the cream using your mixer. When the mixture is creamy, add the coriander seed followed by the honey. Add the honey one tablespoon at a time until the taste of the dip is as sweet as you like it. This is a matter of individual taste. Serve the dip at room temperature with your favorite crackers.
Makes enough for a large dip dish.

mushroom-yoghurt dip

2 tablespoons butter
4 ounces finely-chopped
  mushrooms
4 scallions, chopped using 2
  inches of the greens
3 ounces cream cheese
½ cup unflavored yoghurt
1 small garlic clove, crushed
1 teaspoon salt
Parsley for garnish

Sauté the mushrooms and scallions in butter until golden-brown. Allow to cool to room temperature.

Cream the remaining ingredients in a bowl blending until smooth. Add the mushroom and scallion mixture. Sprinkle with salt and mix well, adjusting the seasonings if necessary. Mound onto your serving dish and refrigerate until well-chilled. Garnish with parsley. Makes about 2 ½ cups.

cheese and herb spread

Serve this spread with party rye or any of the thin, middle eastern breads. Good for cocktails or as a first course.

6 ounces cream cheese at room
  temperature
1 cup finely-crumbled Feta
  cheese
½ cup unflavored yoghurt
2 tablespoons finely-chopped
  chives
2 tablespoons chopped fresh
  dill
2 tablespoons chopped fresh
  mint
Salt to taste
1 small garlic clove, crushed
Tomato slices
Cucumber slices
Black olives
Parsley sprigs

With a fork, mash cream cheese until fairly smooth. Add Feta cheese and yoghurt stirring vigorously with a wooden spoon. When fairly light and fluffy, add the seasonings. Cover and chill the mixture for at least 2 hours. When ready to serve, mound the cheese in the center of a dish. Arrange tomatoes, cucumbers, olives, and parsley around the cheese. Serve with your choice of bread or crackers. Makes 4 servings.

hummus

This Middle Eastern delicacy is popular in the West as a dip. To keep up the flavor of the dish, serve it on triangles of pita bread.

1 or 2 mashed garlic cloves
½ teaspoon salt
¼ teaspoon black pepper
¼ teaspoon paprika
⅛ teaspoon cayenne pepper
2 cups cooked garbanzo beans or chick peas (canned chick peas may be substituted, drained and rinsed and liquid reserved)

½ cup tahini (sesame seed paste)
¼ cup lemon juice
Reserved liquid from beans as needed
1 tablespoon olive oil
½ teaspoon paprika
Minced parsley

In a bowl, mash garlic, salt, black pepper, paprika, and cayenne pepper. Drain garbanzo beans reserving the liquid and in a separate bowl mash thoroughly. Gradually, add the garlic mixture along with tahini and lemon juice. Put in as much of the reserved liquid as needed to make a smooth puree, but not too runny. (Hummus should be a spreadable consistency.) Spoon into a serving bowl and pour olive oil and paprika on top. Sprinkle with parsley and your appetizer is ready. Makes 2 to 2½ cups.

turkish stuffed peppers

This is a delicious appetizer and a cook's delight since it can be made ahead and kept in the refrigerator until ready to eat.

⅓ cup olive oil
2 cups chopped onions
1 cup uncooked rice
¼ cup pine nuts
2¼ cups water
1 scant tablespoon tomato paste
1 teaspoon salt
½ teaspoon freshly-ground black pepper

1 teaspoon sugar
1 teaspoon allspice
1½ tablespoons fresh chopped mint
2 tablespoons lemon juice
8 sweet green peppers, tops removed, seeded but kept whole
1 cup water
2 lemons, quartered

In a large skillet, tan the onions in oil. Add the rice and cook for just 3 minutes until rice is well-coated with oil. Stir in pine nuts for 1 minute more. Add water, tomato paste, salt, pepper, sugar, and allspice. When mixture is at a boil, cover and simmer for 30 minutes.

With a large fork, toss rice gently and add mint and lemon juice, tossing again.

Stuff the prepared peppers with the rice and place in a large casserole dish, top-side up. Pour in 1 cup of water and cover the dish. Bake at 350°F for 1 hour or until the peppers are tender. Remove from the oven and allow to cool. Pour off any water that remains and chill the peppers overnight. Serve garnished with the lemon quarters. Makes 8 servings.

shrimp pâté à la egypt

½ pound cooked prawns of shrimp
¼ cup almonds, chopped, toasted and blanched
1 tablespoon grated candied ginger
¼ teaspoon curry powder
1 mashed garlic clove
1 tablespoon fresh lemon juice
2 tablespoons finely-chopped parsley
2 tablespoons melted butter
4 finely-chopped Greek olives
Salt and pepper to taste

garnish: Whole cooked prawns
Lemon wedges
Greek olives

This mixture can be made with a food chopper but is easier in a blender. Puree all ingredients in order given and blend into a smooth paste . Form into a loaf and chill for at least 12 hours, overnight is even better. When ready to serve, place loaf on serving dish and garnish with whole prawns, lemon wedges, and Greek olives. Serve with your favorite cracker or pita bread. Makes one large loaf.

pickled vegetables

This dish serves as a vegetable accompaniment to the meal or as an appetizer when forks are used. The nice part is it can be made well ahead of when you want to use it. It must be made at least 4 to 6 weeks ahead to taste the best.

1 head cauliflower, cut into florets
Celery, cut into 2-inch pieces
1 cabbage, cut into thin wedges
1 large bunch carrots, cleaned and quartered
Wide-mouth quart jars with new lids
1 garlic clove per quart jar
3 quarts water
2 cups white vinegar
1 cup coarse non-iodized salt
6 to 8 crushed dried hot red peppers
2 teaspoons sugar
2 or 3 sprigs fresh dill

Clean and prepare the vegetables and set aside. Sterilize the quart jars and when cool, place 1 garlic clove into each jar.

In a large saucepan bring remaining ingredients to a boil and allow to continue boiling for 10 minutes. Pack some of each of the vegetables into the jars very tightly. Pour liquid or brine over the vegetables and seal the jars. Store for 4 to 6 weeks before serving. Makes at least 4 to 6 servings.

stuffed zucchini

This appetizer or first course can be arranged on its serving platter early in the day and run under the broiler at the last minute.

4 zucchini, about 4 ½ inches long
1 teaspoon salt
1 cup water
1 cup crumbled Feta cheese
⅓ cup grated gruyère cheese
2 tablespoons flour
1 tablespoon chopped fresh dill
1 teaspoon crushed garlic
Hearty dash of freshly-ground black pepper
¼ cup bread crumbs
2 tablespoons butter

Cook zucchini in salted water until tender, about 15 minutes. Drain and let cool. Slice in half lengthwise and scoop out seeds.

Mix cheeses with flour, dill, garlic, and pepper. Arrange zucchini in an oven dish, cut-side up and dust with pepper. Fill with cheese mixture, sprinkle with bread crumbs and dot with butter. Broil for just a few minutes until cheese mixture is very hot. Serve at once. Makes 8 servings.

soups

almond soup

2 tablespoons butter
1 small onion, chopped (about
 ½ cup)
2 tablespoons flour

1 quart boiling chicken stock
½ cup ground almonds
½ cup heavy cream
Salt and pepper to taste

Melt butter, add onions, and cook until onions are transparent. Stir in the flour. Continuing to stir, add the boiling soup stock. Simmer for 5 minutes. Stir in almonds and simmer for another 20 minutes. Last, add cream and allow all to heat through. Season to taste and serve piping hot. Makes 4 to 5 servings.

lemon-flavored chicken soup

Lemon is a popular flavoring in the Middle East and always available. This variation of chicken soup shows how much a lemon can improve an already good soup.

6 tablespoons rice
8 cups chicken stock
4 eggs
4 tablespoons lemon juice
½ teaspoon curry powder
1 tablespoon parsley

Bring rice and soup stock to a boil and then simmer for 20 minutes or until rice is tender. In a bowl, beat eggs, lemon juice, and curry. When well-blended, stir in 3 tablespoons of clear stock until that is also well-blended. Add the egg mixture to soup and stir for 5 minutes more. Ladle soup into serving bowls, sprinkle with parsley, and serve. Makes 4 to 6 servings.

cold yoghurt and cucumber soup

cold yoghurt and cucumber soup

Since it is not always possible to have fresh mint and fresh dill, this recipe calls for dried. If you are using the fresh leaves, double the amount called for here.

1 medium-sized cucumber
2 cups yoghurt
2 teaspoons white vinegar
1 teaspoon olive oil

1 teaspoon dried mint
¼ teaspoon dried dill weed
1 teaspoon salt
Fresh mint leaves for garnish
Cucumber slices for garnish

Peel cucumber and slice in half lengthwise. Remove the seeds and discard. Coarsely chop or grate the cucumber.

Place yoghurt in a bowl and stir until it is very smooth. Add the remaining ingredients, continuing to blend well with your spoon. Be gentle as you mix the ingredients. Add extra salt if desired and refrigerate the soup for at least two hours. Serve in chilled soup bowls. Garnish with fresh mint leaves, if available and cucumber slices. Makes 3 to 4 servings.

lamb and egg soup

1½ pounds lamb or mutton
2 quartered onions
2 cleaned and diced carrots
2 teaspoons salt
½ teaspoon cayenne pepper
4 cups water
4 tablespoons butter or
  margarine

4 tablespoons flour
4 egg yolks
3 tablespoons lemon juice
4 tablespoons butter
1 teaspoon ground paprika

Remove bones from the meat and then place bones and meat in a heavy soup pot. Add onions, carrots, salt, and cayenne pepper with 4 or more cups water to cover all. Cook for at least 1 hour or until meat is tender. Add extra liquid as needed. When meat is fork-tender, strain off the liquid and reserve.

Mince the meat until fine or put through a meat chopper and then return it to the liquid on a low light on the stove. Mix ½ cup of the liquid with the flour to form a paste. Slowly add this thickening to the soup, stirring all the while.

Beat the egg yolks with the lemon juice until frothy. This is best done with a wisk or a fork. Gradually add the egg mixture to the soup. Remove from heat and stir until well-blended.

Place 1 pat of butter in each soup plate. Pour the soup on top of the butter. Sprinkle paprika into each dish and serve at once.

This soup is popular in Turkey as a dish served at weddings but it makes a party anytime you serve it. Makes 4 to 6 servings.

12

turkish tomato soup

1½ cups unflavored yoghurt
1½ tablespoons olive oil
¼ cup lemon juice
1½ teaspoons curry powder

Pinch of thyme, optional
4½ cups tomato juice
Salt to taste
Chopped chives for garnish (Optional)

Beat the yoghurt in a bowl until very smooth. Add olive oil, lemon juice, curry, and thyme. When well-mixed, gradually add the tomato juice. Season with salt, cover, and chill. When ready to serve, dish into individual bowls and garnish with chives. Makes 4 to 6 servings.

turkish tomato soup

yoghurt soup

matzo balls for soup

yoghurt soup

1 cup cooked barley
3 tablespoons butter
1 cup finely-chopped onion
2 pints plain yoghurt
1 egg
1 tablespoon flour

4 cups chicken broth
4 tablespoons butter
1 cup chopped fresh coriander
  (parsley or mint may be
  substituted)
Salt and pepper to taste
Chopped chives for garnish

Cook barley until tender and set aside. In a skillet, melt butter and brown onions lightly. Set aside.

Place yoghurt in a large soup pot over a very low flame. Gradually stir in the egg and the flour. Add the chicken broth, 1 cup at a time, stirring, until mixture comes to a boil. Add the reserved barley and onions and allow to simmer. When ready to serve, sauté the coriander in butter and add to soup along with seasonings to taste. Stir well and ladle into soup bowls piping hot. Garnish with chives. Makes 6 to 8 servings.

yoghurt and noodle soup

3 cups unflavored yoghurt
1 beaten egg
3 cups chicken or beef broth
1 cup ¼-inch noodles broken
  into small pieces
1 teaspoon salt
3 tablespoons butter
1 medium onion, finely
  chopped
1 tablespoon crushed dried
  mint

In a saucepan, mix yoghurt and egg. Then bring to a boil, stirring constantly in one direction (to prevent curdling). Stir in broth, noodles, and salt. Bring to a boil, reduce heat, and simmer for 10 minutes or until the noodles are tender.

While the soup simmers, melt butter in a small pan. Add onions and sauté until lightly-browned. Stir in the mint. Add this mixture to the cooked soup, stir, and serve hot. Makes 4 to 6 servings.

matzo balls for soup

1 cup matzo meal
½ cup chicken stock
¼ teaspoon ground ginger
2 beaten eggs
4 tablespoons oil or melted
  chicken fat

Four hours before planning to serve, mix the ingredients together and refrigerate. This is to allow all moisture to be absorbed into the balls. Measure out 1 tablespoon of the mixture and roll into a ball, using wet hands for the rolling. Continue rolling balls the size you prefer and put on a plate until all are done. Drop the finished balls into the soup about 30 minutes before dinner is ready. Makes 4 to 6 servings.

yoghurt and rice soup

This soup only takes about 25 minutes to make, which means a good hot start to a meal for almost any cold night.

¼ cup uncooked rice
5 cups chicken or beef stock
1 tablespoon cornstarch
2 cups unflavored yoghurt

2 beaten egg yolks
2 tablespoons fresh, chopped mint
2 tablespoons melted butter

Place rice and stock in saucepan and cook for 20 minutes. In a small pan, make a paste of cornstarch mixed with 2 or 3 tablespoons yoghurt. When smooth, gradually add remaining yoghurt, then egg yolks with a few spoonfuls of hot stock, stirring constantly. When the mixture has come to a boil, add it to the simmering rice and cook for just 2 more minutes. (If the soup is too thick, add a little water to make desired consistency.) Dish into serving bowls, sprinkle with mint and melted butter. Makes 4 to 6 servings.

cold fruit soup

1 cup pitted sour red cherries
1 cup sliced peaches
1 cup pitted plums
1 cup grated green apple
1 cup sugar
6 cups water
1 teaspoon lemon juice
1 stick cinnamon

4 whole cloves
¼ teaspoon salt
1½ tablespoons cornstarch
3 tablespoons water
1 cup half-and-half
3 tablespoons Sabra* or lemon juice
Sour cream

Combine and cook the first ten ingredients for 20 minutes. Be sure the fruit is tender. Discard cinnamon stick and cloves. Force the mixture through a coarse sieve or a food mill.

Dissolve the cornstarch in water and return fruit to pan. Stir in the cornstarch mixture until fruit is slightly-thickened. Last, add half-and-half and Sabra or lemon juice. Chill thoroughly and add more Sabra/lemon juice if needed to taste. Serve in chilled glass dishes topped with a generous spoonful of sour cream. Makes 6 servings.

* Sabra is a liquer which comes from Israel but lemon juice can be a good substitute.

watercress soup

4 medium-sized potatoes, washed but not peeled
Water to cover
2 medium-sized onions, chopped
3 tablespoons butter

2 bunches watercress, chopped
1 teaspoon salt
¼ teaspoon black pepper
1 cup milk
¾ cup yoghurt
Croutons for garnish

Cover potatoes with water and boil in the jackets until done. Reserve 2 cups of the potato water. Peel and dice the potatoes.

Fry onions in melted butter in a large saucepan until tanned, about 5 minutes. Add the potatoes, potato water, watercress, salt, and pepper. Cover and allow to simmer for 5 minutes. Just before serving, add milk and yoghurt and heat but do not boil. Ladle into soup dishes and garnish with croutons. Makes 4 to 6 servings.

lentil soup

1 tablespoon fresh coriander
  leaves
½ teaspoon salt
1 tablespoon cumin
6 cloves garlic
1 tablespoon oil
2 cups lentils (soaked overnight
  in cold water)
Boiling water to cover
4 cups chicken stock
¼ teaspoon black pepper
Pinch of cayenne pepper
1 tablespoon flour mixed with
  enough water to make a
  paste
2 sliced scallions
1 tablespoon chopped parsley

Crush coriander, salt, cumin, and garlic and sauté in hot oil. Add lentils and cover with boiling water. Cook until water evaporates and add more boiling water as needed until lentils soften, about 2 to 3 hours.

Drain lentils. Then put in the soup pot with chicken stock. Season with black and cayenne peppers. Add the flour mixture and stir soup until it thickens. Add scallions to soup and serve. Sprinkle each soup bowl with parsley. Makes 4 to 6 servings.

chilled melon soup

1 large cantaloupe
1 pint half-and-half
1 small chicken breast, boiled,
  boned and finely-minced
2 tablespoons sugar
¼ teaspoon salt
¼ teaspoon cinnamon
3 tablespoons cornstarch
½ pint half-and-half
1 cup Mandorcrema (Almond
  wine)
Yoghurt for garnish

Prepare melon by halving, removing seeds, and chopping the meat fairly fine. Combine melon meat in a saucepan with half-and-half, chicken meat, sugar, salt, and cinnamon. After mixture has come to a boil, simmer for 10 minutes. Then allow to cool and puree to a fine texture.

Dissolve cornstarch in half-and-half and add to the puree. Cook on a low light until mixture is slightly thickened. Add wine and extra milk, if needed. Chill thoroughly and serve topped with a generous spoonful of yoghurt. Makes 4 to 6 servings.

mint soup

1 tablespoon olive oil
1 crushed garlic clove
½ cup fresh mint leaves or
   2 tablespoons dried mint
2 tablespoons cornstarch
½ cup cold water
4 cups chicken soup
Salt and pepper to taste
Dash of cayenne
3 beaten egg yolks

Heat the oil and sauté garlic and mint on a low heat for 8 to 10 minutes. Mash this through a fine sieve. Dissolve the cornstarch in water.

Put chicken soup stock in large saucepan and bring to a boil. Add the sieved mixture, cornstarch and seasonings and cook for five minutes, allowing soup to thicken slightly. Add the egg yolks and stir until well-blended. Serve in individual soup bowls. Makes 4 servings.

orange and lemon soup

This soup peps up those who eat it because of the spicy flavor. It's a cook's favorite as well since it can be put together in a matter of minutes.

1 large onion, finely-chopped
2 tablespoons margarine
2 cups tomato juice
1 chicken bouillon cube
2 cups orange juice
1 cup lemon juice
1 thinly-sliced lime for garnish

In a large pan, sauté the onion in margarine. Add tomato juice and bouillon cube. Bring to a boil, stirring constantly until cube has completely dissolved. Add the remaining fruit juices and simmer for just 3 minutes. Serve at once, garnished with thin slices of lime. Makes 4 servings.

eggs and pancakes

poached eggs with yoghurt

1 cup unflavored yoghurt
1 small garlic clove,
  finely-chopped
1 teaspoon salt
4 large eggs
Salt to taste
Dash of pepper
2 tablespoons melted unsalted
  butter
1 teaspoon paprika

Combine yoghurt, garlic, and salt and divide into 4 ovenproof ramekins. Put the ramekins in a slow oven of 300°F.
Poach eggs on top of the stove and when done, set 1 egg in each ramekin. Sprinkle with salt and pepper to taste. Add paprika to melted butter and spoon some over each egg to add color. Serve at once. Makes 2 to 4 servings.

coucou

coucou

Variations of this egg dish, sometimes called kuku, are served all over the world — and it is tasty and delicious for any meal from brunch to a light supper.

3 tablespoons butter	¼ cup minced parsley
⅔ cup chopped white of leeks	¼ cup finely-chopped
1 large onion, thinly-sliced	green pepper
1 large baking potato, peeled and thinly-sliced	½ teaspoon salt
	¼ teaspoon pepper
2 ripe tomatoes, peeled and thinly-sliced	2 tablespoons butter, cut into bits
2 tablespoons basil	8 beaten eggs

Sauté the leeks and onion in butter until transparent. Lower the flame and then flatten leeks and onions on the bottom of the skillet. Layer the potatoes and tomatoes and cover with basil, parsley, green peppers, and seasonings. Dot this with butter. Pour the beaten eggs over the vegetables and cover. Simmer slowly until eggs are set and top is lightly-browned. Remove from fire and turn onto a heated platter. Makes 4 servings.

mushroom omelet

Mushrooms grow profusely in the Middle East when the rains come — and here, they make the common egg into an omelet delicacy.

2 tablespoons butter
2 cups sliced mushrooms
1 teaspoon fat
4 beaten eggs
4 tablespoons milk
Salt and pepper to taste

Melt the butter and sauté the mushrooms for about 5 minutes. Using another skillet, melt the fat. Mix the beaten eggs with milk and seasonings and pour into the skillet. Cook over a moderate flame until the eggs begin to set and are firm. Lay the mushrooms on half of the eggs and fold over on top of the other half. Remove to a heated platter and serve at once. Makes 3 to 4 servings.

mushroom omelet

squash omelet

2 yellow squash, about 6 inches long
4 eggs
4 tablespoons water
Generous dash of salt
3 tablespoons butter
1 medium onion, finely-chopped
Salt and pepper to taste

Wash and dry squash and trim off the ends. Cut into ¼-inch slices and then cut slices in half.

In a bowl, beat eggs, water, and salt.

Use a medium skillet to sauté the onion in butter until onion is transparent. Add the squash and cook together for 15 minutes. Salt and pepper the squash. Pour the egg mixture over the squash and cook over low heat. Lift edges to allow uncooked egg to run out. When the omelet is set, cut into 4 sections and remove from the skillet to warmed plates. The omelet should be moist on top to be just right. Makes 4 servings.

vegetable and herb omelet

6 well-beaten eggs
½ cup finely-chopped spinach leaves
¼ cup chopped leek with some greens
¼ cup chopped scallions with some greens
1 cup finely-chopped parsley
¼ cup chopped fresh dill
¼ cup fresh chopped mint
2 tablespoons finely-chopped fresh coriander
2 tablespoons chopped walnuts
2 tablespoons currants
1 teaspoon salt
½ teaspoon black pepper
2 tablespoons butter
1 cup unflavored yoghurt

After the eggs are well-beaten, add remaining ingredients except for butter and yoghurt. Mix well.
Melt the butter in an ovenproof dish. Pour in the egg mixture. Bake covered at 350°F for 30 minutes. Uncover and bake until eggs are set, about 25 minutes. When the top forms a golden crust, dish and serve with yoghurt on the side. Makes 4 servings.

yoghurt pancakes

yoghurt pancakes

4 egg yolks
¼ cup sugar
2 cups unflavored yoghurt
4 tablespoons melted butter
1½ cups flour
2 teaspoons baking powder
1 teaspoon baking soda
1 teaspoon salt
3 stiffly-beaten egg whites

Add all of the ingredients in the order given, lastly gently folding in the beaten egg whites. Drop by tablespoons onto a hot griddle. Turn once to brown both sides of the pancake. Remove finished ones to a heated platter and keep warm until all are finished. Serve at once. Makes 4 to 6 servings.

22

meat

turkish meat loaf

Skin from 3 or 4 large
   eggplants
4 tablespoons olive oil
3 pounds lean lamb or beef,
   ground twice
2 grated onions
2 cups seasoned croutons,
   soaked in milk and squeezed
   dry
½ cup minced parsley
½ cup minced green pepper

2 minced garlic cloves
2 beaten eggs
½ cup grated Kefalotyri or
   Parmesan cheese
3 tablespoons olive oil
½ cup tomato sauce
1 ½ teaspoons salt
½ teaspoon freshly-ground
   black pepper
Melted butter to brush over top
   of mold

Line a buttered bundt pan with the skins of eggplant which have been
tenderized in fat in a skillet for 3 minutes. (Save the scooped out pulp of
the eggplants for salad.) Reserve some skins to cover the meat mixture.

Combine and mix the remaining ingredients thoroughly. Press this mixture
into the lined mold and cover with remaining skins. Brush generously with
melted butter.

Place in a large pan of hot water. Bake for 1 hour at 350° F. Let stand for 5
to 10 minutes and then turn out onto a platter. You may add your favorite
white sauce or tomato sauce to cover but it is not really needed. The dish is
delicious as is. Makes 8 to 10 servings.

stuffed melon

Although this recipe came from an Armenian friend, it can be made in any part of the world when melons are available.

1 melon (honeydew, Persian, or
   cantaloupe)
½ pound ground lamb or beef
1 medium-sized onion, chopped
2 tablespoons margarine
1 cup cooked rice
⅓ cup currants
⅓ cup pignolias (pine nuts)
⅓ cup sweet white wine or
   water

Cut off enough of the top of the melon to remove all seeds and some of the flesh. Leave a layer of flesh in the fruit.

Lightly sauté the meat and onion in the margarine. Add rice, currants, and pine nuts, as well as the scooped out melon. Stir until all is well-blended. Fill the melon with the well-blended mixture and put on a baking pan. Pour the white wine into the melon.

Bake at 350° F for 50 minutes to 1 hour, adding liquid if needed. Cut into 4 servings by slicing melon from top to bottom.

veal with kadota figs

8 4-ounce slices veal
6 tablespoons flour
¼ pound butter
3 cups chicken stock
¼ cup sweet sherry
1 cup chopped mushrooms
¼ cup chopped parsley, fresh
   preferred
1 tablespoon tomato paste
1 tablespoon lemon juice
½ cup sour cream
1 small can Kadota figs

Prepare veal by dredging each slice on both sides in the flour. Melt butter in a skillet and fry veal slices until golden-brown on both sides. Place the veal slices in a casserole and reserve the juices in the pan. To those drippings, add chicken stock and remaining flour from the dredging. Stir until smooth and thickened. Add remaining ingredients except for the figs and keep stirring. When all have been added, pour the sauce over the veal and bake at 350° F for 1 hour.

When ready to serve, drain figs and rinse under cold water. Arrange them on top of the casserole and serve with pride. Makes 4 to 6 servings.

okra-lamb casserole

This Middle East combination has many virtues. It can be prepared in the morning and baked before serving. The cook can be a hostess while the dinner is in the oven.

2 large onions, minced
1 minced garlic clove
1 tablespoon minced parsley
6 tablespoons butter
2 pounds ground lean lamb (or beef)
½ teaspoon salt
Healthy dash of pepper
1 teaspoon oregano (fresh preferred) or
1 tablespoon minced fresh mint
½ teaspoon ground coriander (optional)

3 tablespoons tomato paste
1 16-ounce package frozen okra, defrosted and drained
4 tablespoons butter
½ cup bread crumbs
2 well-beaten eggs
4 tablespoons burnt butter
3 tablespoons lemon juice
Butter to dot the top

Sauté onions, garlic, and parsley in butter. Add and brown the meat with salt, pepper, oregano (or mint), and coriander. Spoon in tomato paste and simmer until the juices are absorbed. Set aside.

Sauté okra in butter until vegetable begins to soften. Then set aside.

Add bread crumbs and eggs to the meat. Put in a well-greased casserole and top with burnt butter. Then arrange the okra on top of the meat. Pour lemon juice over all and dot with butter. Cover and bake at 350° F for 45 minutes. Serve from the casserole with your favorite pilaf. Makes 6 to 8 servings.

lamb with orange and barley

This easy entree can be prepared in the morning and put in the oven 1 ½ hours before serving. It takes a minimum of preparation and is delicious.

2 tablespoons oil
2 medium onions, chopped
2 cups diced cooked lamb
1 cup pearl barley
3 unpeeled oranges sliced in thin rounds and seeded
1 tablespoon lemon juice
3 cups beef broth

In oil, lightly brown the onions with the diced, cooked lamb. Place in a casserole dish with barley, oranges, lemon juice, and 1 cup beef broth. Cover and place in 300° F oven for 15 minutes. Add 1 more cup beef broth and cover again. Bake for 30 minutes more. Add last cup of beef broth and bake for 45 minutes more. Remove from oven and allow to stand covered for 10 minutes and then serve. Makes 4 servings.

cauliflower with lamb cubes

½ pound lamb cut into 1-inch
  cubes
4 tablespoons margarine
1 4-ounce can tomato puree
1 cup water
2 packages frozen cauliflower,
  thawed
Salt and pepper to taste

Brown lamb cubes in margarine. Add tomato puree and water and stir well over low heat for 5 minutes. Add the drained, thawed cauliflower, uncooked, to the meat. Salt and pepper to taste and cook for 5 more minutes or until cauliflower is tender. Serve at once. Makes 4 servings.

lamb with lemons

¼ cup olive oil
⅛ teaspoon ground ginger
¼ teaspoon saffron (optional)
½ teaspoon salt
2 pounds boneless lamb, cut
  into 1½-inch cubes
3 cups water
1 ½ cups chopped onions
1 finely-minced garlic clove
6 crushed coriander seeds
2 quartered and seeded lemons
16 green olives

Use a large skillet and blend oil, ginger, saffron, and salt. When fat is hot, add lamb cubes stirring until meat is browned. Add water, onions, garlic, coriander, and lemons. Meat should be covered so add more water if necessary. Bring all to a boil and then reduce heat and simmer for 1 hour until meat is tender. Remove meat and continue cooking liquid until it is only 3 cups. Then return meat to skillet. Add olives and heat for 5 minutes. Add extra salt if desired. Makes 4 servings.

lamb and spinach stew

1 chopped onion
1 chopped garlic clove
1 tablespoon butter
2 cups diced lamb
½ teaspoon allspice
Salt and pepper to taste
2 cups water
1 pound fresh spinach, washed
  and drained
Lemon slices for garnish

In a large skillet, sauté onions and garlic in butter until onions are transparent. Add the diced lamb, seasonings, and water and simmer until lamb is tender, about 45 minutes. Last, add the spinach and simmer for 20 minutes more. Transfer stew to serving platter and garnish with lemon slices. Makes 4 servings.

variation of skewered lamb

lamb kebabs

1½ pounds chopped lamb
1 finely-chopped onion
1 tablespoon chopped parsley
1 teaspoon salt
¼ teaspoon pepper
1 quartered onion
1 quartered tomato
¼ cup oil to brush kebabs

Grind the meat and onion twice. To this, add parsley, salt, and pepper. Form into long, thin fingers and alternate the meat fingers, onion quarters, and tomato quarters on skewers. Brush or drip oil over the kebabs and grill, preferably on an open fire. Remove from skewers and serve on a bed of rice. Makes 4 to 6 servings.

lamb stew

2 pounds cubed boneless lamb
4 tablespoons butter
1 cup minced onions
2 finely-minced garlic cloves
½ teaspoon salt
¼ teaspoon pepper
½ teaspoon nutmeg
½ teaspoon allspice
½ teaspoon cumin
½ teaspoon paprika
½ cup white wine
1 8-ounce can tomato sauce
¼ cup minced parsley
1 pound small pearl onions
½ cup white wine

Sauté lamb cubes in butter with onions and garlic cloves until meat is browned on all sides. Add salt, pepper, and other seasonings. Stir wine, tomato sauce, and parsley into the mixture. Add pearl onions and pour the other ½ cup of white wine over all. Cover and simmer for 45 minutes or until lamb is tender. If needed, add extra water during this time.

This stew is good if served over hot rice but best over eggplant base for stew (see index). Makes 6 to 8 servings.

skewered lamb

¼ cup minced onion
1 minced garlic clove
3 tablespoons olive oil
3 tablespoons lemon juice
1 teaspoon salt
¼ teaspoon pepper
½ teaspoon crumbled dried
   oregano
1½ pounds leg of lamb or
   lamb shoulder meat, cut into
   2-inch cubes
16 small boiling onions, peeled
15 mushrooms, cleaned and
   stems removed
2 red peppers, cut into chunks

Combine the onion, garlic, olive oil, lemon juice, salt, pepper, and oregano in a glass bowl or casserole. Add the lamb cubes and stir well. Cover and marinate for 3 to 4 hours (or longer in the refrigerator), stirring occasionally.

Parboil the onions in salted water for 10 minutes. Drain and cool.

Drain the lamb, reserving the marinade. Skewer the vegetables and lamb alternately (lamb cube, onion, mushroom, and then a pepper chunk; repeat). Cook over charcoal or in the broiler about 15 minutes, brushing frequently with the marinade.

Serve with rice. Makes 4 servings.

variation

Substitute cherry tomatoes and green peppers for the red peppers. Skewer the onions and meat alternately. Skewer the vegetables separately, and brush them with marinade. Tomatoes can be grilled only a short time or they will fall off the skewer before the meat is done. Start the meat first and add the skewered vegetables 5 minutes before the meat is finished.

egyptian veal

4 tablespoons margarine
½ teaspoon salt
Few grains saffron
2 tablespoons lemon juice
2 pounds boned veal
1 cup water
1 small chili pepper

Cream margarine, salt, and saffron until smooth. Pour lemon juice over the meat slowly and then spread the meat with the creamed mixture. Put the meat in a heavy saucepan or deep skillet. Add water and chili pepper and bring to a boil. Then simmer the meat for 1 hour, basting every 15 minutes or so. When ready to serve, the meat will be fork tender and delicious. Makes 4 to 6 servings.

poultry

cinnamon stick chicken

The hidden ingredient in the tasty sauce is cinnamon. It makes chicken taste like a party.

1 3-to-3½ pound chicken cut
    into pieces
Salt
Dash of freshly ground pepper
4 tablespoons butter
1½ cups finely-chopped onions
    (2 medium onions)
1 tablespoon chopped garlic
6 plum tomatoes, peeled,
    seeded and finely-chopped or
1 cup canned plum tomatoes,
    chopped and drained
2 tablespoons tomato paste
½ cup chicken stock
2 cinnamon sticks

Season chicken pieces with salt and pepper. Melt butter in a large skillet. Add chicken, skin-side down and turn until brown on all sides. Brown a few pieces at a time. When all are done, set aside.

Pour off most of the fat and add onions and garlic, stirring until onions are lightly-browned. Add remaining ingredients with more salt and pepper if needed. When liquid has come to a boil, add the chicken, being sure that each piece is basted in the sauce. Cover and reduce heat. Simmer for 30 minutes, remove chicken to platter, and spoon the sauce over it. Serve at once. Makes 4 servings.

stuffed roast chicken

stuffed roast chicken

4 tablespoons butter
½ cup finely-chopped onions
Giblets (liver, heart, and
    gizzard) of the chicken
    coarsely-chopped
2 tablespoons pine nuts
1 cup uncooked long-grain
    white rice

2 cups water
1 tablespoon dried currants
2 tablespoons salt
Freshly-ground pepper to taste
4 tablespoons melted butter
3- to 3½-pound roasting
    chicken
3 tablespoons yoghurt

Melt butter in a large suacepan, add onions and cook until transparent, about 5 minutes. Add giblets and pine nuts and stir together for 2 minutes more. Then stir in rice until the grains are covered with butter. Add water, currants, 1 tablespoon salt, and pepper and allow all to come to a boil. Reduce heat, cover, and simmer for 30 minutes or until rice has absorbed all of the liquid. Remove from the heat and stir in the melted butter, lifting gently with a fork.

Thoroughly dry the chicken inside and out and stuff with 1 cup of the rice mixture. Close all openings and truss the chicken securely. (Set aside the remaining rice to be heated and served when the chicken is finished cooking.)

Combine yoghurt with remaining tablespoon of salt. Use half of this mixture to coat the chicken thoroughly. Place chicken, breast-side up, on roasting pan and roast at 400°F for 15 minutes. Baste chicken again with remaining yoghurt mixture and continue cooking, lowering oven to 350°F, for 1 hour. When chicken is done, put on a heated serving platter and serve along with the heated rice bowl. Makes 4 to 6 servings.

broiled chicken with cucumber sauce

This makes a great hot-weather meal, since it is light and refreshing and easy on the cook.

¼ cup olive oil
¼ cup lemon juice
1 cup dry white wine
1 teaspoon crumbled dried
   oregano

1 broiler-fryer (approximately
   2½ pounds), split and
   quartered

Combine the oil, lemon juice, wine, and oregano and pour over the chicken in a baking dish. Marinate at room temperature for 3 hours. Broil in the oven 4 inches from the heat source, turning once, and basting with the marinade, until done (may also be broiled over charcoal). Serve with Cucumber Sauce. Makes 4 servings.

cucumber sauce

1 cup plain yogurt
⅓ cup olive oil
1 peeled and crushed garlic
   clove

1 teaspoon salt
1 peeled, seeded, and finely-
   chopped cucumber

Combine the yoghurt, olive oil, garlic, salt, and cucumber and serve over the chicken.

chicken with rice and cherries

1 3-pound chicken cut into
   serving pieces
Salt and pepper to season
   chicken
4 tablespoons olive oil
2 medium onions, finely-sliced
½ cup chicken stock

2-pound can stoned black
   cherries, drained
¼ cup sugar
2 tablespoons water
¼ pound melted butter
2 cups cooked long grained rice

Sprinkle the chicken with salt and pepper. Heat oil in large skillet and brown chicken pieces, a few at a time. Transfer cooked chicken to a heated plate. Then fry onions in oil until lightly-tanned, about 5 minutes. Return chicken to skillet, add chicken stock and bring to a boil. Reduce heat, cover and simmer for 30 minutes. Transfer chicken to a plate, reserving liquid.

Make a sauce of cherries, sugar, and water, simmering for 5 minutes and stirring frequently. Remove from the heat and set aside.

Add half the melted butter to the reserved liquid. Put in half of the rice on a low heat and cook for about 5 minutes until rice is evenly-coated. Transfer rice mixture to a casserole dish. Cover with chicken pieces and about half the cherries. Add rest of rice and melted butter and pour remaining cherries and their liquid over all.

Bake covered, at 350° F for 20 minutes or until all are piping hot. Serve at once. Makes 4 to 6 servings.

chicken with sesame seeds

½ cup flour
Salt and pepper to taste
1 teaspoon paprika
2 3-pound chickens cut into
  pieces
3 tablespoons oil
2 tablespoons light brown sugar
½ teaspoon ground ginger
1 cup dry red wine
2 tablespoons soy sauce
⅓ cup sesame seeds

Combine flour, salt, pepper, and paprika in a brown paper bag and coat the chicken pieces thoroughly by shaking them in the bag. Heat the oil in a skillet and brown the chicken, setting each piece in a casserole when done.

To the remaining fat, add brown sugar, ginger, wine, and soy sauce. Stir and when well-blended, pour over the waiting chicken. Sprinkle with sesame seeds which have been lightly toasted in a dry skillet.

Bake at 350°F for 1 hour. Makes 6 to 8 servings.

moroccan chicken

This simple dish has many variations, all of which are good. Serve on a bed of plain noodles with a salad.

¼ cup olive oil
1 4-pound chicken, skinned and
  cut into serving pieces
1 medium-sized onion,
  thinly-sliced into rings
2 crushed garlic cloves
1 teaspoon salt
1 teaspoon black pepper
½ teaspoon oregano
1 bay leaf
2 tablespoons lemon juice
1 ¼ cups chicken stock
1 teaspoon cornstarch

Heat oil on moderate heat and brown the chicken pieces, turning them to brown on all sides. When chicken is nicely-browned, drain on paper towels. Cook only as many pieces as the pan will hold. Do not crowd.

Pour off all but 2 tablespoons of oil. Add onion and garlic and cook until onion is golden, stirring occasionally. Add remaining seasonings and chicken stock. When liquid has come to a boil, return chicken to pan. Cover and simmer for 1 ½ hours or more until chicken is tender.

Transfer chicken to a heated platter. Strain the remaining liquid into a small saucepan, pressing the seasonings down to extract all the liquid. Dissolve cornstarch in ¼ cup of the liquid and add. Stir constantly until the mixture has thickened. Pour over the chicken pieces and let your dinner begin. Makes 4 to 6 servings.

lemon-flavored chicken wings

The flavor of lemon is strong in this chicken dish but it is tender and good, especially if served with a sweet rice dish.

**2 pounds chicken wings (about
   12 wings)
2 cups lemon juice
1 teaspoon salt
½ teaspoon black pepper
4 tablespoons butter or
   margarine**

Cut off the smallest wing tip of the chicken wings and save for soup. You will only use the meaty pieces of the wings here. Make a marinade of lemon juice, salt, and pepper and place wings in a bowl with marinade covering. Marinate the chicken for 24 hours, stirring from time to time so that all pieces are covered.

When ready to cook, drain chicken on paper towels. Place in pan and rub each piece liberally with butter. Broil for 15 to 20 minutes or until crisp, or place in a hot oven at 500°F for ½ hour to 45 minutes. Makes 4 to 6 servings.

baked rice with chicken

In this recipe, rice is the mainstay with chicken as an accompanying flavor. The molded rice well-turned-out makes a dinner into a party.

**4 tablespoons softened butter
3 cups uncooked white rice
4 boned and halved chicken
   breasts
Salt and pepper
1½ cups milk
1 cup heavy cream
4 cups chicken stock
2 tablespoons butter, cut into
   pieces for dotting**

Heavily grease the bottom and sides of a 3-quart casserole or baking dish. Use all 4 tablespoons of the butter. Spread 1 ½ cups uncooked rice in the dish. Place chicken, skin-side up, on top of rice and season with salt and pepper.

In a saucepan, bring milk, cream, and 2 cups of stock to a boil. Pour over the chicken. Cover with remaining rice and dot with butter. Bake uncovered in a 400° F oven for 15 minutes. Simmer the remaining 2 cups of stock. Pour 1 cup over the casserole and bake for 15 minutes more. Pour in the remaining stock and bake for 30 minutes.

Remove casserole from oven and cover tightly, allowing to stand at room temperature for 20 minutes. Use a sharp knife around the inside edges of the casserole to loosen and allow to rest for 10 minutes more. Place a heated serving platter over the top of the casserole and invert. The molded rice will slide out easily and you will be called a gourmet cook. Makes 6 to 8 servings.

chicken with yoghurt

3 pounds fryer-chicken parts
Juice of 1 lemon
Salt and pepper
6 tablespoons butter
2 minced garlic cloves
2 medium onions, sliced
½ cup white wine
1 cup chicken broth
1 teaspoon crumbled rosemary
1 cup plain yoghurt
2 tablespoons flour

Rub the chicken with the lemon juice, salt, and pepper.

Melt the butter in a large, heavy skillet. Brown the chicken on all sides. Add the garlic and onions and brown them lightly. Add the wine, chicken broth, and rosemary. Reduce the heat to low, cover, and cook for 30 minutes or until the chicken is tender.

Combine the yoghurt and flour and mix well.

Remove the skillet from the heat and allow to cool for 10 to 15 minutes. Add the yoghurt and flour slowly, mixing well. Cook, stirring constantly, over very low heat until slightly thickened.

Pour the sauce over the chicken and serve. Makes 4 servings.

chicken liver pilaf

5 tablespoons butter
1 tablespoon olive oil
1 large onion, sliced
½ pound chicken livers
10 small scallions, cut into
   ½-inch lengths
1 tablespoon pine nuts
1 tablespoon raisins
1 ½ teaspoons salt
½ teaspoon black pepper
2 cups long-grain rice, soaked
   in cold water for 30 minutes
2 teaspoons sugar
2 teaspoons lemon juice
1 tablespoon tomato puree
1 teaspoon dried dill
2¾ cups boiling water

In a skillet, melt 2 tablespoons butter and oil. Add onions and stir for 4 minutes. Add chicken livers and sauté until liver is brown on all sides, stirring constantly. Stir in scallions, nuts, raisins, salt, and pepper. Cook for 3 minutes more. Remove from the pan and set aside.

Melt remaining butter in a large saucepan. Add rice and stir until well-coated, about 5 minutes. Add the remaining ingredients in order given. When all comes to a boil, reduce heat and cover. Cook for 20 minutes or until rice is tender with all liquid absorbed. Serve while hot. Makes 4 servings.

fish

stuffed bass

1 3-pound bass
Salt and pepper
1 tablespoon butter
2 large onions, grated
½ cup finely-ground almonds
1 teaspoon sugar
½ teaspoon cinnamon
¼ teaspoon cumin
2 tablespoons sweet butter
2 tablespoons almond paste
3 tablespoons quince preserves
½ cup water
Lemon wedges and parsley for
  garnish

Sprinkle fish inside and out with salt and pepper. In a skillet, sauté the onions in butter until onions are transparent. Layer this on the bottom of a baking dish.

Make a paste of the almonds, sugar, cinnamon, cumin, sweet butter, almond paste, and preserves. Spread this onto the fish with a spatula until all fish is covered with a smooth paste. Then put the fish on top of the onions and pour water around but not over the fish. Bake at 350° F for 45 minutes or until fish is fork tender. Garnish with lemon wedges and parsley. Makes 4 to 6 servings.

deep-fried fish balls

deep-fried fish balls

1 pound fresh fish fillets
2 large potatoes, sliced
Salt water
1 beaten egg
1 teaspoon minced onion
½ teaspoon salt
¼ teaspoon black pepper
½ teaspoon dry mustard
1 teaspoon lemon juice
2 tablespoons parsley
Oil for deep frying

Place fish and potatoes in salt water to cover and cook for 20 minutes until both are tender. Drain well. Place drained fish and potatoes in a large bowl and stir gently to mix them. Add the egg, onion, salt, pepper, mustard, lemon juice, and parsley. When all are mixed well, form into balls about 2 inches in diameter. Heat oil for deep frying and drop balls, frying until golden-brown. Remove cooked balls to a heated platter. When all are finished, serve at once. Makes 4 servings.

deep-fried cod

deep-fried cod

2½ pounds salt cod
3 cups flour
2 cups lukewarm water
½ teaspoon baking soda
½ teaspoon salt
Oil for deep frying
Lemon wedges for garnish

A day ahead, put cod in a glass pan or bowl, cover with cold water, and soak for at least 12 hours, changing the water 3 times. When ready to cook, drain and rinse cod under water and cut into pieces 2 inches × 1 inch.

With a wooden spoon, combine 2 cups flour, water, baking soda, and salt mixing until creamy. Let batter mixture stand for 1 hour at room temperature.

Heat fat in deep fryer. Dip fish, one piece at a time, into remaining cup of flour. Drop into liquid batter and when coated on all sides, deep fry for 5 minutes or until golden-brown. Keep finished pieces warm in the oven. When all are done, transfer to serving platter and garnish with lemon wedges. Makes 4 servings.

baked fish greek-style

4 fish fillets	**2 cups canned tomato sauce**
Lemon juice	**⅓ cup chopped parsley**
Salt and freshly-ground black pepper	**1 teaspoon oregano**
⅛ teaspoon cinnamon	
⅓ cup olive oil	**⅓ cup sweet red wine**
3 large onions, chopped (about 3 cups)	**⅓ cup grated bread crumbs**
	2 tablespoons butter

Rub fish slices with lemon juice and wash. Then season well with salt and pepper and let stand for 10 minutes.

Sauté onions in olive oil in a skillet for 5 minutes or until transparent. Add tomato sauce, parsley, oregano, cinnamon, and wine. Cover and cook for 10 minutes.

In a greased baking dish, arrange the fish and pour sauce over it. Sprinkle the surface with the bread crumbs and dot with butter. Bake at 350° F for 30 minutes or until a nice crust has formed over the fish. Serve at once. Makes 4 servings.

fish in ginger sauce

The original recipe called for 4 fillets of sole — and that is always good. However, any fresh fish fillets will do as well as frozen fillets when fresh is not available.

4 fillets of fish, preferably sole
3 chopped scallions
1 tablespoon oil
2 tablespoons tahina (sesame
   sauce)
2 tablespoons soy sauce
½ teaspoon freshly-grated
   ginger
2 cups water
2 tablespoons cornstarch
¼ cup water
Salt to taste

Place fillets in baking dish and bake for 20 minutes at 350°F. While they are baking, sauté scallions in oil for 5 minutes. Add tahina paste, soy sauce, ginger, and 2 cups of water. While this is heating, make a paste of the cornstarch in ¼ cup of water. Add to the sauce stirring until thickened. Taste and add salt. Simmer together for about 10 minutes or until fish is done. Pour the sauce over the fish and serve at once. Makes 4 servings.

fish in ginger sauce

fish with vegetables and yoghurt

1 sliced onion
1 sliced green pepper
1 peeled and chopped tomato
1¼ pounds fish fillets
1 minced garlic clove
½ teaspoon oregano

½ teaspoon salt
¼ teaspoon pepper
3 tablespoons butter
1 cup plain yoghurt or sour
   cream

Place half of the vegetables on the bottom of a greased baking dish. Top with the fish fillets. Sprinkle with the oregano, salt, and pepper. Top with remaining vegetables and dot with the butter. Bake at 350°F for 30 minutes.

Top the dish with the yoghurt, and cook 10 minutes more. Makes 4 servings.

fish in curry sauce

2 pounds of your favorite fish
Salt
½ cup pine nuts
4 tablespoons oil
1 cup water
2 tablespoons lemon juice

1 tablespoon chopped parsley
1 teaspoon curry powder
Dash of cayenne
Dash of freshly-ground black
   pepper

After washing the fish and drying on paper towels, sprinkle with salt and allow to stand for ½ hour. Just before you are ready to cook the fish, wash it again and dry as before.

Put the pine nuts in heated fat and let brown lightly. Brown the fish quickly on both sides. Place fish in a greased oven dish. Combine remaining ingredients and pour over the fish. Bake at 350° F until the sauce is absorbed, about 30 minutes. Makes 4 to 6 servings.

persian sturgeon

2 pounds sturgeon cut into
   1½-inch chunks
3 tablespoons olive oil
2 tablespoons lemon juice
2 tablespoons minced fresh dill
   weed
Paprika to taste

Marinate the sturgeon chunks in olive oil, lemon juice, and dill weed for at least 20 minutes. Drain and reserve the marinade.

Place the fish chunks on skewers and sprinkle liberally with paprika. Broil quickly, basting often with reserved marinade for at least 10 minutes per side. When fish is tender, but not overcooked, remove from skewers and serve. This is particularly good served with a pilaf. Makes 4 servings.

skewered swordfish

Happy memories of this delicacy served in Washington D.C. made it a must for this book. The hostess was Scandinavian, the host was American and the entree recipe came from Turkey.

**1 small onion, thinly-sliced and
  separated into rings
4 tablespoons fresh lemon juice
4 teaspoons olive oil
2 teaspoons salt
½ teaspoon freshly-ground
  black pepper
1½ pounds swordfish, skinned,
  boned and cut into 1-inch
  cubes
2 cups boiling water
20 large bay leaves**

Prepare a marinade of onions, 2 tablespoons lemon juice, 2 teaspoons olive oil, salt, and pepper. To this, add the fish, coating each cube well. Marinate for 4 hours in the refrigerator stirring occasionally. Soak the bay leaves in boiling water for 1 hour.

When ready to cook, drain bay leaves and layer cubes of fish and bay leaves alternately on skewers. Combine remaining lemon juice and oil and brush onto the fish. Place skewers in a roasting pan and broil for 8 to 10 minutes, turning once, until fish is lightly-browned. Remove from skewers and serve at once. Makes 4 servings.

vegetables

burghul

This side dish is a substitute for the starch of your meal. In the Middle East, it is often used in place of rice.

1 cup burghul (cracked wheat)
4 tablespoons oil
2 cups soup stock
Salt and pepper to taste

Sauté the burghul in oil until well-covered. Add the soup stock and seasonings and lower the flame to a simmer. Allow to cook until the liquid is all absorbed, about 2 hours. Add extra salt and pepper if needed. Serve at once. Makes 4 servings.

cabbage and sour cream

6 cups finely-shredded cabbage,
  (1 medium head)
4 tablespoons butter
1½ teaspoons salt
1½ teaspoons lemon juice
2 tablespoons sugar
1 egg
1 cup sour cream

Over a low heat, sauté cabbage in butter for 45 minutes. Stir frequently so it doesn't stick to the pan. Add salt, lemon juice, and sugar and cook 5 minutes longer. Combine the egg and sour cream in a bowl, beating until the egg disappears. Gradually add to the cabbage while stirring until all begins to thicken. Serve at once topped with additional sour cream, if desired. Makes 4 to 6 servings.

eggplant base for stew

2 large eggplants
1 cup white sauce (cream of celery soup can be used)
Salt and pepper to taste
2 tablespoons butter

¼ cup pine nuts
Minced parsley
Green pepper rings for garnish
Lemon wedges for garnish

Broil eggplants until skins are blackened and pulp is fork tender. Peel and drain pulp thoroughly. Then place pulp in a deep bowl and mash to a fine consistency. Add a cup of white sauce and salt and pepper, continuing to whip. Mound on a heated platter and make a well in the center with a spoon.

Heat butter and pine nuts until nuts are golden-brown. Then put nuts in the well of the eggplant. Sprinkle with parsley and garnish the platter with pepper rings and lemon wedges.

This dish is good with any entree but particularly tasty with lamb stew. Makes 6 to 8 servings.

falafel

Falafel, although a staple food in Israel, is also used as a filler for pita bread and many times as an hors d'oeuvre. Prepared according to this recipe, it can be a starchy vegetable as well.

½ pound fresh chickpeas
Water
3 tablespoons burghul (cracked wheat)
2 tablespoons flour
2 crushed garlic cloves

1 teaspoon salt
Dash chili pepper
1 teaspoon ground cumin
Pinch of ground coriander
Oil for deep frying

Cover the chickpeas in water and soak overnight. Soak burghul in water for 1 hour. Put both chickpeas and burghul through the meat grinder. Add flour and seasonings and then mix thoroughly. Form the mixture into small balls about 1½ inches in diameter.

Deep-fry the balls in oil until lightly-browned. Drain on paper towels and keep warm until all balls are fried. Serve at once. Makes about 30 balls.

basic pilaf

Pilaf can have as many different flavorings as there are cooks but this is a good basic recipe. You make your own variations.

4 tablespoons butter
1 cup long-grain rice
2 cups hot chicken broth
1 teaspoon salt

Melt butter in a skillet and sauté the rice until the grains are translucent. Stir in the two cups of hot broth and salt. Bring to a boil and cover. Reduce heat to a simmer and allow rice to cook without lifting the lid for 20 minutes. Remove from heat and leave covered for another 15 minutes. Just before serving, toss the pilaf with a fork to separate the grains so that they are light and fluffy. Makes 4 to 6 servings.

stuffed cabbage

1 large head cabbage, with
  center core removed
Boiling water to cover
1 cup uncooked long-grain rice
½ cup minced onions
1 well-beaten egg
2 tablespoons parsley
2 tablespoons olive oil

2 tablespoons tomato sauce
1 minced garlic clove
1 teaspoon salt
1 teaspoon minced mint leaves
½ teaspoon allspice
½ teaspoon black pepper
¼ cup or more olive oil
4 to 6 cups chicken broth

Place cabbage in large pot with the core on the bottom of the pot. Cover with boiling water and allow to boil for 5 minutes. Remove, drain, and allow to cool until able to handle. Separate the leaves of the cabbage and set aside.

In a bowl, combine rice, onions, egg, parsley, olive oil, tomato sauce, garlic, and seasonings. Mix well. This is the stuffing mixture.

At the core end of the cabbage leaves, place about 1 tablespoon of the stuffing. Roll the leaf once and then fold in the ends, envelope-style. Roll the rest of the leaf until stuffing is well-covered. Continue to do this with the leaves until all stuffing is used.

In a heavy saucepan, layer the remaining cabbage leaves. Cover with the cabbage rolls placed seam-side down. Sprinkle the first layer of rolls with olive oil and some chicken broth. Proceed in this way with the layering until all of the stuffed rolls are in the pan. When all rolls are used, cover with chicken broth. Cook on a low flame for 1 hour on until leaves are tender and the rice done. Remove to a heated platter, pour some of the liquid over all and serve. Makes 6 servings.

stuffed cabbage

turkish eggplant

turkish eggplant

4 small eggplants
3 tablespoons vegetable oil
2 medium onions, sliced
3 peeled and sliced tomatoes
2 minced garlic cloves
½ teaspoon salt
1 tablespoon chopped parsley
1 bay leaf
1 cinnamon stick
⅛ teaspoon white pepper
8 black olives
8 rolled anchovy fillets

Remove stems and approximately ½-inch slice from top of eggplants (see picture).

Heat 2 tablespoons of the oil in a frypan and fry eggplants on all sides for 5 minutes. Remove eggplants from pan, cool slightly, and scoop out pulp, leaving a shell approximately 1-inch thick.

Heat 1 tablespoon oil in same pan, add onions, and sauté lightly. Stir in tomatoes and simmer for 5 minutes. Return diced pulp to frypan. Add garlic, salt, parsley, bay leaf, cinnamon stick, and white pepper. Cook for another 5 minutes; remove bay leaf and cinnamon.

Arrange eggplant shells in a greased baking dish and fill with vegetable mixture. Bake in a preheated oven, 350° F for 15 minutes. Garnish with olives and anchovies. Makes 4 servings.

potato latkes

Potato pancakes are particularly popular in Israel during the Jewish festival of Hannukah but they are enjoyed whenever they are served.

6 medium potatoes, peeled and grated	Dash of ginger or nutmeg (optional)
½ teaspoon baking soda	½ cup flour
2 grated onions	1 teaspoon salt
2 eggs	Dash of black pepper
	Fat for deep frying

Sprinkle the grated potatoes with the baking soda. Spoon out most of the excess liquid. Add the remaining ingredients in the order given.

Heat the fat in a large skillet and drop batter by spoonfuls to form potato cakes about 4 inches in diameter. When crisp on both sides, remove and drain on paper towels. Keep warm until all are cooked and then watch them disappear at the table as everyone enjoys them. Makes 6 to 8 servings.

spinach pie

½ package prepared filo leaves
  (about 16, 12 by 15 inches)
4 tablespoons butter
½ cup finely-chopped onions
3 10-ounce packages chopped
  spinach, thawed and drained
3 eggs
½ pound crumbled Feta cheese
¼ cup chopped parsley
2 tablespoons chopped fresh dill
1 teaspoon salt
Hearty dash of freshly-ground
  pepper
¼ cup melted butter

Allow filo leaves to come to room temperature. In medium skillet, melt butter and sauté onions until golden, about 5 minutes. Add spinach and stir well. When blended, remove from the heat.

Beat the eggs with a rotary beater. Then use a wooden spoon to stir in cheese, parsley, dill, salt, pepper, and spinach mixture. Mix well.

With some of the melted butter, grease a 13- by 9- by 2-inch baking pan. Layer 8 of the filo leaves in the bottom of the dish, brushing the top of each with melted butter before adding the next leaf. When 8 leaves have been brushed with butter, spread the spinach mixture evenly. Then cover with 8 more leaves, again brushing each leaf with butter. If any butter remains, pour over the top of all.

Trim off any rough edges using a scissors. Then take a sharp knife and cut into squares before baking. Bake at 350° F for 30 minutes or until top crust is puffy and golden. Serve warm. Makes 8 to 10 servings.

Tip for the cook: cover filo leaves not being used with damp paper towels to prevent drying out and to make them easier to handle.

lentil and spinach pilaf

This dish is filling enough to be served by itself as a meatless dinner or can accompany the meat of your choice as a vegetable — good either way.

3 tablespoons butter
1 pound spinach, washed, dried
  and chopped
1 minced garlic clove
1 ½ cups cooked lentils
1 tablespoon chopped parsley
½ teaspoon salt
¼ teaspoon pepper
¼ teaspoon cumin
1 recipe basic Pilaf (see index)
3 tablespoons melted butter

Melt butter in skillet and sauté the spinach and minced garlic until it is wilted. Add the lentils, parsley, and seasonings and sauté together for about 5 minutes or until all are blended and heated through. Taste to add extra seasonings if needed. Put onto a heated platter and top with the pilaf. Cover with melted butter and serve. Makes 4 to 6 servings.

noodle kugel

A good noodle kugel has as many variations as there are cooks. Put in whatever you like and it's sure to please. The recipe here is a basic recipe for a sweet kugel.

8 ounces cooked and drained
  broad noodles
1 cup cottage cheese
1 cup sour cream
4 beaten eggs
1 cup sugar
1 ½ teaspoons cinnamon
¼ cup raisins or currants,
  optional
½ cup chopped nuts, optional

Place cooked and drained noodles in a large bowl. Using a wooden spoon to mix, stir in the rest of the ingredients as given. Place this mixture in a greased 9- by 13-inch baking dish. Bake at 350°F for 30 to 45 minutes until noodles on top are lightly-tanned. Serve hot. Makes 6 to 8 servings.

stuffed grape leaves

1 medium-size jar of grape leaves
1 cup of rice
¼ cup of boiling water
1 grated onion
1 bunch chopped green onions
1 teaspoon salt
1 teaspoon pepper
1 teaspoon dill
1 tablespoon dry mint
½ cup oil
¼ cup chopped parsley

Wash the grape leaves with water and set aside. Soak the rice in boiling water until it absorbs the liquid. Add onions, seasonings, and ¼ cup of the oil and stir well.

Take a grape leaf and place 1 teaspoon of the mixture in the center. Wrap well. When all are wrapped, place the grape leaves in a saucepan. Pour remaining ¼ cup of oil and 1 ½ cups water over them. Bring to a boil, then cover, reduce heat, and simmer for 40 minutes. Serve with lemon sauce and egg. Makes 4 to 6 servings.

lemon sauce with egg

2 eggs
Juice of 1 lemon
½ cup broth from grape leaves
½ cup water

Beat eggs with wisk until frothy and add lemon juice. Add ½ cup broth from the grape leaves and ½ cup water. Stir this mixture over low heat until it thickens. Pour over the stuffed grape leaves.

stuffed grape leaves

pharaoh's wheel

This recipe came from an Israeli friend and is a holiday dish in Israel. Each ingredient is symbolic of the events in Exodus. The sauce is the Red Sea, the raisins are the Egyptians, and the white pine nuts are their horses.

½ pound narrow egg noodles
2 ½ cups meat gravy
6 ounces thinly-sliced salami
½ cup raisins
½ cup pine nuts

Cook noodles in boiling water for 9 minutes and drain. Grease a 2-quart casserole dish. Alternate layers of noodles, gravy, salami slices, raisins, and nuts. Top the casserole with noodles and decorate with last slices of salami. Bake at 400° F for 15 to 20 minutes. Makes 4 to 6 servings.

salads

egyptian-style white beans

This vegetable is listed as a salad as it is usually served chilled. Whatever you call it, it is filling and tasty on a warm evening.

1½ cups dried white beans	½ cup olive oil
Water to cover	¼ cup lemon juice
3 thinly-sliced scallions	2 finely-minced garlic cloves
1 large cucumber, peeled and thinly-sliced	2 teaspoons salt

Wash beans, cover with water and soak for at least 12 hours; overnight is fine. Drain, place in a pot, and cover with fresh water. Boil for 2 hours or until the bean skins are split. Drain thoroughly and allow to cool.

In a bowl, place beans and remaining ingredients, stirring well to mix all of the flavors. Chill for several hours before serving. Makes 4 to 5 servings.

burghul salad

1 pound burghul (cracked wheat)	Salt and pepper to taste
Enough water to cover	½ cup olive oil
¼ cup chopped mint leaves	6 tablespoons lemon juice
¼ cup chopped parsley	Lettuce or grape leaves
1 bunch chopped scallions	2 tomatoes for garnish (optional, but good)

Wash and drain the burghul and soak in water to cover for 1 hour. Drain again. Add the remaining ingredients (except for lettuce) in order given, mixing thoroughly. Spoon onto a bed of lettuce or grape leaves and chill until served. Garnish with tomato wedges, if desired. Makes 6 servings.

cheese salad

1 small cucumber
Salt
½ cup small-curd cottage
   cheese
½ cup crumbled Feta cheese
1 small onion, grated and
   drained (about ¼ cup)
1 tablespoon minced green
   pepper
¼ cup lemon juice
¼ cup olive oil
Salt and pepper to taste
Sprigs of fresh mint for garnish

After peeling the cucumber, cut in half lengthwise and score with a fork. Sprinkle with salt and set aside for ½ hour.

Mix thoroughly the two cheeses, grated onion, green pepper, lemon juice, and oil. Season to taste with salt and pepper. Then, drain, rinse, and cube the cucumber. Mix into the cheese until well-blended. Divide into individual portions and decorate with the fresh mint. Refrigerate for at least 30 minutes before serving. Makes 4 servings.

easy chickpea salad

2 10-ounce cans chickpeas
½ cup olive oil
3 tablespoons vinegar
1 tablespoon lemon juice
Salt and pepper to taste
1 finely-minced garlic clove
1 medium onion, chopped
1 cup chopped vegetables
   (celery, tomatoes, peppers)
2 tablespoons diced pimentos
   for garnish
Parsley for garnish

Heat the chickpeas and drain. Mix the oil with vinegar, lemon juice, salt, and pepper. Add garlic and onions. Toss all with the chickpeas. Last, add the vegetables, tossing very gently. Decorate the salad with pimentos and sprinkle all with parsley. Makes 4 servings.

cucumbers with feta-cheese dressing

2 thinly-sliced cucumbers
2 large onions, thinly-sliced and
   divided into rings
Lettuce leaves
¼ pound Feta cheese
3 tablespoons olive oil
1 teaspoon minced fresh
   oregano
1 tablespoon lemon juice
Salt and pepper to taste

Arrange the cucumbers and onions on beds of lettuce leaves. Combine the remaining ingredients in the blender to make the dressing. Pour the dressing over the vegetables just before serving. Makes 4 to 6 servings.

eggplant salad

The trickiest part of this salad is the first step. Once that is mastered, you will serve with pride a Middle East dish, which is, with some variations, made from Lebanon to Syria.

1 large eggplant
1 garlic clove, cut in half
1 grated onion
3 tablespoons minced parsley
2 tablespoons minced fresh
   mint
2 tablespoons vinegar
¼ cup olive oil
Salt and pepper to taste
2 ripe tomatoes, cut in eighths
Garnish of fresh sprigs of mint

Hold the eggplant over an open flame until the skin is crisp and the inside soft to the touch. Remove and discard the skin and drain pulp. Dice the drained eggplant.

Rub the salad bowl with garlic. Put diced pulp in bowl. Add onion, parsley, mint, vinegar, olive oil, salt, and pepper. Mix together gently. Chill. Before serving, toss in tomato wedges. Then garnish with mint. The salad is ready and delicious. Makes 4 to 6 servings.

leek salad

1 pound leeks, cleaned, rinsed,
   and drained
Water to cover
1 teaspoon salt
1 tablespoon cornstarch
2 tablespoons lemon juice
2 tablespoons olive oil

Cover leeks with water and add salt. Cook for 15 to 20 minutes or until tender. Drain off liquid and set leeks aside. Add cornstarch to 2 cups of the drained liquid stirring until mixture thickens. Add lemon juice and oil. When blended, pour over the waiting leeks. Allow to cool and then chill thoroughly. The leeks may look like onions, but they taste like asparagus. Makes 3 to 4 servings.

pea-cheese salad

¼ pound diced mild cheddar
   cheese
½ cup mayonnaise
⅓ cup sweet pickles
2 cups drained, canned peas

Thoroughly coat the cheese with mayonnaise in a large bowl. Add the pickles and peas and mix lightly until all are blended but not broken. Marinate for several hours before serving. Makes 4 servings.

radish salad

1 tablespoon lemon juice
6 tablespoons olive oil
½ teaspoon hot mustard
4 to 5 cups thinly-sliced
  radishes, white or red
8 to 10 thinly-sliced black olives
1 cup crumbled Feta cheese

2 tablespoons minced fresh
  parsley
1 thinly-sliced small red onion
Freshly-ground black pepper to
  taste
Salt to taste

Combine lemon juice, oil, and mustard and mix well. (A small jar is good for this. Shake vigorously to mix.)

Place radishes, olives, Feta cheese, parsley, and onion in salad bowl. Add dressing and black pepper and toss well. Add extra salt if needed. Chill for 2 to 4 hours and serve. This salad is a great help when there is a large crop of fresh garden radishes to use up. Makes 6 to 8 servings.

cold spinach salad

2 large bags fresh spinach,
  washed and coarsely chopped
1 large onion, grated
¼ cup water
2 cups well-beaten plain
  yoghurt
2 tablespoons olive oil
1 tablespoon lemon juice
½ teaspoon salt

¼ teaspoon black pepper
1 finely-minced garlic clove
½ cup chopped walnuts
1 tablespoon toasted sesame
  seeds
2 tablespoons minced fresh
  mint
Lemon wedges for garnish
Extra yoghurt, if desired

Place spinach, onion, and water in a large saucepan and cover. Steam for just 5 minutes. Strain through a colander and place spinach mixture in a salad bowl. Add the yoghurt, olive oil, lemon juice, salt, pepper, garlic, and walnuts and mix thoroughly. Adjust seasonings to taste and chill.

When ready to serve, sprinkle salad with sesame seeds and mint and garnish with lemon wedges. Extra yoghurt may be served with the salad for those who prefer more. Makes 4 to 6 servings.

tahina-cheese salad

¼ cup prepared tahina
1 finely-chopped green onion
½ pound creamed cottage
  cheese
2 tablespoons sour cream

Salt and pepper to taste
6 medium cucumbers
Dash of paprika
Lettuce
Tomato slices for garnish

Blend tahina, onion, cottage cheese, sour cream, and seasonings. Set aside.

Slice the cucumbers in half lengthwise. Scoop out the seeds with a teaspoon, chop, and add to the cheese mixture. Fill the cucumber boats with the cheese mixture and sprinkle with paprika. Serve on lettuce and garnish with tomato slices. Makes 12 servings.

breads

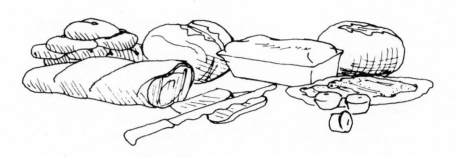

greek new year's bread

This cake is traditionally served at midnight on New Year's Eve. The head of the household cuts the cake and the lucky family member getting the coin is said to have good fortune in the coming year.

⅓ cup sugar
4 tablespoons butter
½ teaspoon salt
½ cup milk
1 package active dry yeast
¼ cup warm water (105 to 115°F)
1 teaspoon ground cardamom

2 beaten eggs
3 to 3 ¼ cups all-purpose flour
Silver coin wrapped in foil
1 egg, beaten with 1 tablespoon water
Sesame seeds
Blanched almonds

Combine the sugar, butter, salt, and milk in small saucepan. Heat just until the butter melts. Cool to lukewarm.

In a large mixing bowl dissolve the yeast in the warm water. Add the milk mixture, cardamom, and eggs and beat until combined. Add 1½ cups of the flour and beat for 5 minutes. Stir in enough of the remaining flour to form a soft dough.

Knead on a floured surface for 10 minutes or until smooth and satiny. Form into a ball. Place in an oiled bowl. Rotate the dough to grease the surface. Cover with a towel and let rise in warm place until doubled in bulk.

Punch down the dough. Let rise again until almost doubled in bulk.

Punch down the dough again. Form into a 9-inch-round cake, placing the foil-wrapped silver coin in the loaf. Place on a greased cookie sheet. Cover and let rise until doubled in bulk.

Brush with the egg and water mixture, sprinkle with sesame seeds, and decorate with blanched almonds. Bake at 375° F for 25 minutes or until golden-brown. Makes 1 9-inch-round loaf.

syrian sesame biscuits

These hard biscuits should be crisp and golden when served and make a delightful change from your normal bread.

3 cups flour
1 teaspoon baking powder
½ cup water
1 beaten egg

2 tablespoons cooking oil
1 tablespoon salt
½ cup sesame seeds

In a large bowl, mix all ingredients in the order given. Roll out the dough, using extra flour if needed, and cut into rounds. Bake in a slow oven at 375°F for 15 minutes to a half hour. Biscuits are done when they are crisp and gold. Makes 12 to 24 biscuits.

lovash bread

Most Middle Eastern breads have similarities and differences. This Armenian recipe is comfortable to make and tastes good as well.

¼ cup warm water
1 package dry yeast
5 cups flour
2 teaspoons salt

2 cups warm milk
1 tablespoon sugar
¼ pound melted butter

Dissolve yeast in warm water and set aside. Combine flour and salt in a large mixing bowl and make a well in the center. Into this well, pour the remaining ingredients and stir with a wooden spoon. You may want to finish the mixing process with your own well-floured hands. Transfer dough to a floured board and knead, adding more flour if needed, until smooth and elastic. Place dough in a greased bowl, turning it to grease the whole ball. Cover and set aside to rise for at least 3 hours.

Divide the dough into 4 parts. Work with 1 part at a time leaving remaining dough covered in bowl. Roll each part out into thin ovals or rounds and place on an ungreased baking sheet. Bake at 350°F for about 25 minutes or until lightly-browned and crisp. Break off pieces to eat with your favorite stew or the dip of your choice. Makes 4 large rounds.

pita

Pita can be found all over the Middle East and varies slightly from place to place. Since it rolls out easily, the baker can decide whether to make paper-thin pitas with a cracker-like consistency or slightly thicker ones which can be split and filled with the preferred filling.

2 packages active dry yeast
2 teaspoons sugar
1¼ cups lukewarm water

4 cups flour
1 teaspoon salt

Place dry yeast and sugar in the water and stir until well-dissolved. Add the flour and salt. When all is well-mixed, knead the dough generously for 5 minutes. Then divide the dough into equal parts to make 18 or 20 balls. Roll out each ball on a floured board to about 5 inches in diameter and ¼ inch thick. (If you prefer thinner pita, roll some more.) Let the pitas rise in a warm place for ½ hour or until puffy. Bake a few at a time in a 500°F oven for no more than 5 minutes or until they get puffy. Pitas are particularly good served with a dip — but this useful bread has any number of other uses — all good. Makes 18 to 20 pitas.

challah

challah

The Challah is the traditional Sabbath bread in Jewish homes. No representative cookbook of the Middle East would be complete without it — and the taste is very special.

¾ cup milk	¼ cup warm water
¼ pound butter	4½ cups sifted flour
⅓ cup sugar	2 beaten eggs
½ teaspoon salt	1½ tablespoons lemon juice
1 package dry yeast	1 beaten egg for topping

Warm milk, butter, sugar, and salt in a saucepan until butter has melted. Set aside to cool. Mix the yeast in warm water until dissolved.

Place flour in large bowl. Add milk mixture, yeast, eggs, and lemon and mix thoroughly with a wooden spoon. Knead the dough on a floured board until smooth. Let dough rise at least 2 hours in a greased, covered bowl.

Punch down dough on floured surface. For 1 large loaf, divide dough into 3 equal parts. Roll each part into a long strip. When there are 3 strips, join them at one end and braid, being sure to seal the edges at each end. Place twist on a greased sheet or in a 9- by 13-inch pan. Brush over the entire top with reserved egg and set aside to rise for at least 1 hour more.

Bake 10 minutes at 325° F and then 30 to 35 minutes more at 350° F. Cool on a rack. Serve with pride. Makes 2 small loaves or 1 large twist.

yoghurt bread

1½ cups warm water
2 packages active dry yeast
1 cup unflavored yoghurt at
   room temperature
1 tablespoon salt
About 5 cups flour

Pour water into large mixing bowl and sprinkle yeast on top. Allow to rest for 5 minutes. Stir to dissolve yeast. Add yoghurt and salt. Stir in 3 cups of flour, beating with a wooden spoon until smooth. Add remaining flour a little at a time and knead the dough in the bowl until it is no longer sticky. Then remove to a floured surface and knead until dough is stiff. Place ball in a lightly-greased bowl turning once and cover. Let rise in a warm place until doubled in bulk — at least 1 ½ hours.

Punch down dough and divide into 2 parts. Shape each into a long or round loaf. Place shaped bread in baking dish. Cover and allow to rise again for another hour or until doubled in size. Make an X mark on top of each loaf about ½ inch deep. Brush loaves with water.

Bake at 400° F for 45 minutes or until crusts are golden-brown. Brush with water twice during baking period. Makes 2 loaves.

yemenite bread

6 cups flour
1 teaspoon salt
1 package dry yeast
3 cups water

Mix flour and salt. Dissolve the yeast in ¼ cup of the water. Add the yeast mixture and remaining water. Set aside to rise for 2 hours or more.

Roll out the dough on a floured board. The thinner the dough is rolled, the more cracker-like the finished product will be. You may prefer to divide the dough out into 3 or 4 balls before rolling to make large ovals or rounds. When dough is rolled thin, place on a greased baking sheet and bake at 450° F for about 5 minutes if very thin, longer as needed. The amount made depends on how thin the dough is rolled.

feta-cheese sandwiches

2 pita-bread rounds
8 ½-inch slices Feta cheese
1 cup finely-shredded lettuce
½ of a medium tomato, diced
¼ cup diced cucumber
2 tablespoons chopped green
   pepper
2 thinly-sliced radishes
3 tablespoons oil-and-vinegar
   salad dressing

Warm the pita bread. Cut in half and form a pocket in each. Place 2 slices of cheese in each pocket.

In a bowl combine the vegetables and salad dressing.

Stuff each bread pocket with some of the salad mixture, and serve. Makes 2 servings.

pocket sandwiches

2 tablespoons olive oil
1 pound ground beef or lamb
½ cup chopped onion
¼ cup chopped green pepper
½ cup tomato sauce
½ teaspoon salt
¼ teaspoon pepper
½ teaspoon crumbled dried
   oregano
4 pieces pita bread

Heat the olive oil in a medium-size skillet. Add the ground meat and sauté for 5 minutes. Add the onion and green pepper and sauté for 3 more minutes. Drain off the fat. Add the tomato sauce and seasonings. Cover and simmer for 5 minutes.

With a knife split the pita-bread pieces one-fourth of the way around and make a pocket. Stuff the bread with the meat mixture. Makes 4 servings.

desserts

apples and whipped cream

1 cup sugar
1 cup water
16 whole cloves

4 peeled and cored cooking
  apples
½ cup stiffly-whipped heavy
  cream

Use a saucepan large enough to hold the apples, about 4 quarts. Stir sugar and water together until the sugar is totally dissolved.

Insert 4 cloves on the top of each apple. Put the apples, clove-side up, in the syrup and baste. Reduce the heat and allow to simmer for 15 minutes, basting occasionally. When apples are tender, remove from the heat and allow to come to room temperature.

Place apples in individual dessert dishes and cover with a dollop of whipped cream. Pour 1 tablespoon of syrup over all and serve with pride. Makes 4 servings.

apricot delight

1 cup dried apricots
1½ cups water
2 tablespoons apricot preserves
⅓ cup sugar
3 slivers lemon peel

½ teaspoon grated orange peel
1 cup heavy cream
1 cup topping of slightly-
  sweetened whipped cream
Chopped nuts for garnish

Combine apricots, water, preserves, sugar, lemon peel, and orange peel in a saucepan. Bring to a boil and then simmer for 25 minutes. Cool and puree in a blender or put through a food mill. Whip the cup of heavy cream until stiff and fold into the cooled mixture. Fill serving glasses with this. Chill. When ready to serve, top each portion with the slightly-sweetened whipped cream. Garnish with chopped nuts, if desired. Makes 4 to 6 servings.

greek nut pastry

honey syrup

1 small lemon	1 2-inch piece cinnamon stick
1 cup sugar	4 whole cloves
1 cup water	1 cup honey

Remove the zest from the lemon (the thin yellow skin only, not the white pith). Squeeze 1 ½ teaspoons of lemon juice from the lemon and set aside. Combine the lemon zest, sugar, water, cinnamon stick, and cloves in a heavy saucepan. Bring to a boil. Lower the heat and continue cooking without stirring for 25 minutes. The mixture should be syrupy (230° F on a candy thermometer). Stir in the honey and pour through a strainer into a pitcher or measuring cup. Add the lemon juice. Stir and allow to cool.

pastry

½ pound melted sweet butter	1 cup finely-chopped almonds
1 pound filo sheets	½ cup sugar
1 cup finely-chopped pecans	1½ teaspoons ground
1 cup finely-chopped walnuts	cinnamon

Brush a 13- by 9- by 2-inch baking dish with some of the melted butter. Fold a filo sheet in half and place in the dish. Brush with butter and top with another folded sheet of filo and brush with butter.

In a small bowl, combine the pecans, walnuts, almonds, sugar, and cinnamon and mix well. Top filo with ½ cup of the nut mixture. Top with 2 more folded sheets of filo, brushing each with butter. Top with ½ cup of nuts. Continue layering 2 folded sheets of filo (buttering each) and nut mixture until 2 sheets of filo remain. Fold, butter, and layer them to form the top crust.

With a razor blade, cut the top layers into 24 small rectangles. Bake at 325°F for 50 minutes. Remove from the oven and with a sharp knife cut through all the layers of pastry, using the top layers as a guide, to form individual rectangles.

Pour the cooled syrup over the pastry and cool. Cover and let stand overnight. Makes 24 pieces of pastry.

avocado dessert

4 medium avocados
6 teaspoons lemon juice
¼ cup sugar
3 tablespoons sour cream
1 tablespoon liquer

Peel and seed ripe avocados and press the meat through a sieve or mash very fine with a fork. Add the remaining ingredients and mix very well. Chill thoroughly. When ready to serve, spoon into dessert dishes and top with extra sour cream, if desired. Makes 6 to 8 servings.

egyptian palace bread

½ pound honey
½ cup margarine
½ cup sugar
1 cup (or more) white bread
    crumbs

Heat honey, margarine, and sugar in a pan until all are melted and mixed together. Add the bread crumbs stirring constantly until the mixture is one mass, cooking for about 5 to 10 minutes. Put onto a plate and allow to cool, spreading out fairly flat, about ½ inch thick. When cool, cut into individual cakes. Makes 4 to 6 servings.

figs in yoghurt

Fresh figs, abundant in the Middle East, have a delicious flavor all their own. However, canned figs may be substituted here and will still make an elegant dessert.

12 peeled fresh figs (do not peel
    canned figs)
½ cup chopped blanched
    almonds
12 whole blanched almonds
1 cup almond brandy or fruit
    wine

1 pint yoghurt
1 tablespoon honey
¼ teaspoon vanilla
Crushed, blanched almonds for
    garnish

Open each fig and stuff with the nuts. Cover the stuffing with 1 whole almond. Place figs in a shallow dish and pour brandy or wine over them to almost cover the fruit. Let figs stand in this marinade for several hours. Then remove figs, reserving the liquid.

Combine the reserved liquid with yoghurt, honey, and vanilla. Divide the mixture and pour into 4 chilled compotes. Place three figs in each glass and sprinkle with garnish. Chill until time to serve and enjoy. Makes 4 servings.

melon and peach delight

1 medium Persian melon or
    2 small cantaloupes
½ teaspoon salt
2 fresh peaches, peeled and cut
    into ½-inch slices

½ cup sugar
3 tablespoons lemon juice
2 tablespoons rose water

Halve the melon and remove and discard seeds. Using a melon baller, scoop out as many balls as possible. If you prefer, with a knife, cut the fruit into ¾-inch squares, as this uses all of the melon. Put melon into a bowl and squeeze out the juice remaining in the rind. Discard the shells. Sprinkle the fruit with salt.

Prepare the peaches and add to the melon. Dissolve sugar in lemon juice and rose water and pour over the fruit, stirring gently to combine all flavors. Cover and refrigerate until thoroughly chilled. Serve in individual glass dishes so the color of the fruit pleases the eye as the taste pleases the palate. Makes 4 to 6 servings.

shortbread cookies

If you have a Syrian "S"-shaped cookie cutter, you can make these into that shape. If not, cut them into rectangles — they will taste good either way.

1 cup butter
½ cup sugar
4 cups flour
Blanched almonds

Mix butter, sugar, and flour, adding the flour last and gradually so all is well-blended. Pat the dough out onto a floured board. Cut into rectangles and top each one with a blanched almond. Bake at 350°F for about 30 minutes. Dust with confectioner's sugar, if desired. Makes 24 to 36 cookies.

yoghurt cake

1 18-ounce yellow cake mix
4 eggs
½ cup vegetable oil
1 cup plain or lemon-flavored
  yoghurt
½ teaspoon lemon extract
1 teaspoon grated lemon peel
1 teaspoon ground cinnamon
1 cup chopped walnuts

Grease and flour a 1-inch tube or fluted pan.

In a large mixing bowl, combine cake mix, eggs, oil, yoghurt, lemon extract, lemon peel, and cinnamon. Blend until moistened. Beat for 2 minutes.

Add the nuts and mix just until combined. Pour into the prepared pan. Bake at 350°F for 60 minutes or until done. Cool 10 minutes and then turn out on a rack to cool. Slice and serve. Makes 16 servings.

sweet rice

This rice is in the dessert section but it is also a pleasant accompaniment to lemon-flavored chicken wings. Any way you use it, this rice is good.

5 cups rice
8 cups water
1 cup sugar
2 teaspoons cinnamon

½ teaspoon grated lemon rind
⅓ cup chopped dates
1 cup chopped walnuts
½ cup chopped pine nuts

Place the rice, water, sugar, cinnamon, and lemon rind in a large saucepan. Bring to a boil and then reduce flame to a medium heat. Stirring constantly, allow all to cook for 20 minutes. When rice is tender, add dates and heat through for just 3 more minutes. Place rice in serving bowls and garnish with walnuts and pine nuts. Makes 4 to 6 servings.

carrot cake

1½ cups flour
1½ cups sugar
1 teaspoon baking powder
1 teaspoon salt
½ teaspoon baking soda
½ teaspoon cinnamon
½ teaspoon nutmeg
½ teaspoon ginger
¾ cup cooking oil
3 eggs
3 teaspoons hot water
1 cup cooked, mashed carrots
  (canned will do)
½ cup walnuts
Powdered sugar
Marzipan carrots (optional)

Mix dry ingredients together in order given. Add cooking oil, eggs, water, and carrots; stir until well-blended. (Use a wooden spoon — it's easier.) Add walnuts. Pour batter into ungreased cake or tube pan. Bake at 350° F for 45 minutes. Dust with powdered sugar and decorate with marzipan carrots, if desired. Makes 8 to 10 servings.

carrot cake

date-nut loaf

date-nut loaf

Since dates and nuts are prevalent all over the Middle East, this popular cake is made in many countries — and it's always good.

3 cups flour
4 tablespoons baking powder
½ cup sugar
1 teaspoon salt
1 cup chopped dates
¼ cup chopped pecans
1 beaten egg
1½ cups milk
2 tablespoons melted butter
Slivered nuts (optional)

Place dry ingredients in a large bowl and add the dates and nuts. Beat egg, milk, and butter together and gradually add to the flour mixture. When all is mixed, turn into a buttered loaf pan and allow to stand for 30 minutes. Then bake at 350°F for about 1 ½ hours. Cool the loaf on a rack. Decorate with slivered nuts. Slice to serve—the thinner the better. Makes about 10 slices.

quick-and-easy baklava

Although some baklava calls for filo leaves, which may be substituted here for the puff pastry, this recipe is easier to handle and oh-so-good.

2 packages frozen puff pastry
4 or more tablespoons butter
1 pound coarsely-chopped
   walnuts
1 cup and 2 tablespoons sugar
2 tablespoons lemon juice
Grated lemon peel
3 tablespoons water
1 tablespoon minced
   peppermint leaves

Knead the dough into a ball and then roll out paper-thin. Melt the butter and grease an 8-inch square baking dish. Line the bottom of the dish with a layer of the thin dough. Brush the top with melted butter and sprinkle some of the nuts on top. Continue layers of dough, butter, and nuts until dish is full (about 6 layers). Cover with a final layer of dough. Bake for 45 minutes at 425° F.

Make a thick syrup of the remaining ingredients in a saucepan. Allow to cool slightly. After the baklava has come out of the oven, pour the glaze over it. Divide into portions with a knife and serve either warm or at room temperature. Makes 4 to 6 servings. There usually isn't any of this left over. It's too good!

quick-and-easy baklava

arabian orange custard

½ cup brown sugar
1 tablespoon hot water
2 oranges, peeled and sectioned
   with membrane removed
6 eggs
¾ cup white sugar
3 cups hot milk
½ teaspoon salt

Butter a baking dish and set aside.

Melt the brown sugar in water and cook for 2 minutes.

Place the orange sections in the buttered dish and pour the melted sugar over them. In a bowl, beat the eggs and white sugar together. Gradually add the hot milk and then the salt. Pour this into the dish over the waiting fruit. Place mold in a pan of hot water and bake at 350° F for 50 to 60 minutes. When a knife comes out of the center clean, the custard is done. Allow to cool and then chill for at least 2 hours. Makes 6 servings.

sweet figs

4 cups water
1½ cups sugar
Dash of ginger
Dash of cinnamon
1 pound dried figs
Juice of 1 orange and ½ lemon
Pine nuts for garnish

Make a syrup of the water and sugar and add the spices. (Be generous with spices.) Add figs and cook 10 to 15 minutes until the syrup has thickened. Add the fruit juices and remove from heat. Chill. When ready to serve, spoon into dessert dishes and top with pine nuts. Makes 4 to 6 servings.

grape compote

½ cup sugar
3 cups water
½ cup Concord wine
4 cups grapes

Bring sugar and water to a boil and then add the wine. Bring this mixture back to a boil and then remove from heat. Add the grapes to the hot liquid. No further cooking is needed. When the mixture has cooled to room temperature, put in a bowl and chill. Serve from the chilled bowl and enjoy. Makes 6 to 8 servings.

index

63